© 1994 Sammamish Press,
P.O. Box 895, Issaquah, Washington, 98027
ISBN 0-942381-10-6
Printed and bound in Hong Kong
By Book Art Inc., Toronto

To my son Ryan.
For the child within us all.

THE PUGET SOUND REGION

It is sacred ground, hallowed and sadly beautiful. In the Suquamish Catholic cemetery, Chief Seattle's grave faces his namesake city across Puget Sound. From the dandelion-studded knoll, under the shelter of maples on the Port Madison Indian Reservation, one sees the forest of skyscrapers. An anomaly.

"The white man will never be alone," promised the great Chief—Sealth in his tongue—as he signed the white man's treaty. "At night, when the streets of your cities and villages will be silent and you think them deserted, they will throng with the returning hosts that once filled and still love this beautiful land."

If you are quiet and your spirit alert, you may sense the ancient presence of those who cherished this land, and hear the Smokehouse drums and aching spirit songs that filled the winter nights. Now, the waves of evergreens are frothed with cities and towns of three million people. Though the remnants of tribes who hunted and fished and waged war do indeed "resemble the scattering trees of a stormswept plain," the Indian influence is inescapable.

Native American names and derivations color the region: Puyallup (pew-AL-up), Tacoma, Issaquah, Enumclaw, Snoqualmie, Sammamish, Snohomish, Skagit, and, of course, Seattle. Indian names grace the fleet of ferries that connect one Puget Sound shore to another. "Puget," by the way, is British, after an 18th century explorer Peter Puget. Pronounce it "PEW-jit," *not* "Pudge-it."

The northwesternmost location and strong Native American influence, particularly the newsworthy confrontations over fishing rights and land ownership, lead many outside Washington state to see the region as pioneer country with tomahawks and flying arrows. However, contentious issues are now settled on the legal battleground. Non-Indians are coming to see that the hasty treaties were signed by people who did not understand them. Even many Seattle-area churches have issued a formal apology for misguided destruction of native religion and culture.

Nevertheless, many Puget Sounders would just as soon keep outsiders thinking the worst. Take the weather. It is a cliché, certainly, that Seattleites don't tan, they rust. Drizzly rain, non-stop rain, "vile, thicke and stinking fogges" (in the words of early explorer Sir Francis Drake), make for dreary winters. Tourists who never make it here because the airport is fogbound for two weeks, visitors who spend ten days here and never see "The Mountain," and the unfortunate who visit in November will never, NEVER move here. So it is hoped.

Yet the secret leaks out. While sub-zero temperatures strangle other parts of the country, we are griping about a little rain. When the air-conditioning comes on in Kansas, the mercury tops 115 in Phoenix, and the humidity suffocates Louisiana, we merely open our windows and enjoy perfect soul massages. Like the song says, we *do* have the "bluest skies you've ever seen."

Yeah, so sometimes it rains in summer. We get cheated. Like the cold summer the year that Mount St. Helens erupted. Then there's El Nino—the weather phenomenon caused by the shifting Japanese current—which can bring spring-like Januaries, snowfree mountains and drought. Water conservation and prohibitions on lawn watering are no longer exclusively California happenings.

Such things can be accommodated, and more and more folk are doing just that. More than half the present population was not born in this state. And most who stay come grudgingly to love the soft rain and moody landscapes.

So, what do we care about? Well, quality of living for one. Growth management, wetlands protections, mass transit. We argue about those things. And there's sports: The Cougs and the Dawgs (Washington State Cougars and University of Washington Huskies). The Mariners and the Seahawks and the Sonics. Hydroplanes. We argue about those, too. And about school reform, health care, and whether the state song should be "Louie, Louie."

There are clichés about us. "We" patronize latte' and espresso stands that are as ubiquitous as one-armed bandits in Vegas. "We" are oh so politically correct. "We" are low on church attendance and high on book-buying. "We" wait for walk signals.

And "we" know we live in one of the most extraordinary pieces of earth. Seattle, of course, is the human centerpiece. Few cities are as artfully layered; new skyscrapers—several art deco in style—push up like mushrooms, dwarfing the Smith Tower which at one time was the world's tallest building outside New York. This "Emerald City" was placed in a setting of water, islands and mountain ranges. Its modernistic composition matures gracefully. Whether it is the linear panorama from Alki Point, the compact cluster from Queen Anne Hill, or the eye-popping spread northbound on I-5, Seattle ranks as one of the world's greatest pieces of living, breathing art.

But in another context, Seattle is an anomaly. From a logging road scratched onto a ridge to Mount Juniper in the Olympics, you can see the city across Hood Canal. It's a three-hour trip, across Puget Sound by ferry, over the Hood Canal Bridge, along Highway 101 near Brinnon, up a rutted road and through clearcuts and wild rhododendrons. Far off, Seattle is a zit in the wilderness, an extraterrestrial city. For all its people, its wealth, its monuments to humankind, Seattle is merely a speck of life between two mountain ranges.

And its sister cities are tangent molecules connected by arteries: two Lake Washington floating bridges (one span sank in a recent storm), white ferries that crisscross the Sound, Interstate 5 that sprouts major shopping malls. Businesspeople share downtown Seattle streets with the homeless, and commute to Bellevue, Everett, Bremerton, Tacoma. Or they take a bus to their hip condo or downtown apartment and shop for the evening's dinner at Pike Place Market, or visit the corner vegetable stand in Wallingford, or sip a latte' in Starbuck's while waiting for traffic to thin out.

Tacoma, 35 miles south of Seattle, was almost *the* city back in the days when being a railroad town meant something. Seattleites were furious when the Northern Pacific Railroad selected Tacoma as the western terminus of its operation in 1873. Tacomans boasted that Seattle would soon eat their dust and busied themselves proving it. Tacoma's population increased from 1,100 in 1880 to 36,000 in 1890. But when the Northern Pacific went bankrupt in the Panic of 1893, Tacoma foundered. Seattle held on until the Klondike Gold Rush in the late 1890s. The 1900 census revealed Seattle's population gain of 38,000 people; Tacoma's was reversed to 2,800.

An offshoot of the outright hostility between the sister cities was the controversy over Tacoma's desire to change the name of Mount Rainier back to its Indian name of Tacoma. With typical revolutionary aplomb, the Northern Pacific began printing "Mount Tacoma" on its maps and literature. Historian Murray Morgan, in his book *Puget's Sound*, said, "Seattle took it as a declaration of war."

Insults flew, verbally and editorially, prophetically and posthumously. The United States Geographic Board rendered its opinion in 1890: Rainier it's been for nearly a century, and Rainier it shall remain. If Captain George Vancouver in 1792 could have foreseen the rift his naming of the mountain would cause, he might have sailed back out of the sound he called "Puget". And because Vancouver's friend Rear Admiral Peter Rainier was a British officer during the Revolutionary War, Tacomans had further cause to revile the name.

They continued the fight well into the next century, losing another round with the Geographic Board in 1917 and failing a bid in the legislature. But, oh, the fight was good while it lasted. Seattle and Tacoma newspapers accused each other of greed and envy. Patriotic abuse was at its most creative. And always at the heart of the controversy was The Big Question. Was "Tacoma" *ever* the Indian name for The Mountain? An array of ethnologists, scientists and pioneers planted themselves firmly on either side. Tacomans today generally hold that Tacoma or Tahoma was the original name for The Mountain That Was God, or the "Breast of Milk-White Waters". Many have never forgiven Seattle for "stealing the mountain". Twice in the 1980s the Washington State Board on Geographical Names has declined requests to change the name of the mountain.

Perhaps a truer name would be Mount Rainy. When the mountain wears a cloud cap, precipitation is usually on the way. And if "the mountain is out", it's not raining. People flock to Mount Rainier's sub-alpine meadows, sometimes loving them to death. They camp in its backcountry. Some 7,000 climb its flanks every year; a few are children, blind, on crutches. All challenge the moving glaciers and the evil Tamahnawas that kept the Indians from its summit. Mount Rainier is a sullen mystic in winter, a joyful deity in summer. Hidden in long stretches of winter cover, the peak will burst from its prison in pristine radiance. There is a special kinship with Tahoma, whether it is love from afar, or an affair rekindled in its meadows.

Yet inner fires portend a volcanic awakening. Summit steam caves warm climbers; glacial outbursts (perhaps influenced by volcanic heat) create sudden floods. An eruption would be disastrous; present-day towns are built on mudflows from eruptions thousands of years ago. Perhaps its volcanic life will be like that of Mount Baker, trembling and puffing with harmless bravado. Or maybe the inner fires will slowly die, leaving only glaciers and weather to carve the mountain.

The canvas of the future can be painted within the sketch of the past. No historians watched the top of the mountain collapse in an explosion 5,800 years ago. There were no farmlands in the Puget Sound valleys where the Osceola Mudflow left 70 feet of new soil. Undoubtedly there were Indians who trembled when the mountain spirits breathed fire and smoke and shook the earth. But the enormous forces, the cataclysmic eruptions and mudflows, the grinding glaciers that shaped what is now Mount Rainier National Park are responsible for the beauty of places like Sunset Amphitheater and Paradise Valley. The latter is the most popular spot in the park. A sub-alpine summer there crams the vibrancy of spring and the freewheeling exuberance of a lowland summer into two or three short months. White fields of avalanche lilies push through the July snow. In August they are replaced by a quilt of lavender lupine dotted with red paintbrush and pasqueflower seedheads. Hoary marmots whistle from dens, camp robbers beg for handouts, and butterflies dance over fields like blossoms blown loose. Autumn brings salmon, coral, vermilion, gold, pumpkin. The hues of mountain ash and Cascade huckleberry change with the sunlight. Lit from the rear or side, the dying leaves are aflame. Under overcast skies they become muted, rich and intense. The leaves take on diamond drops in a windless fog. Snows come and go before finally burying the land for another eight months.

Other mountains mark the fringes of the Puget Sound region, but none are as renowned as Mount Rainier. The state's tallest peak is visible to all but those in the northermost reaches of the Sound, the premier landmark in a region of unsurpassed beauty.

Purple lupine and Indian paintbrush are the most prominent decorations in the sub-alpine meadows of Mount Rainier National Park. It is a delicate land where the tread of a foot may cause damage that takes a century to repair. Even in summer, the wind that blows across the glaciers hints of the winter that locks the meadows in eight months of snow. Popular meadow hikes are in Paradise and at Tipsoo Lake.

Mount Rainier reflected in a tarn above Mystic Lake.

(right) Lewis monkeyflower blooms along streambeds in Mount Rainier National Park. Even when the mountain is hidden in clouds, its treasures are near at hand.

Fall means ripe huckleberries and rich color in the meadows of Mount Rainier National Park. Low-growing Cascade huckleberries and taller mountain ash cover the slopes with crimson, scarlet, gold, pumpkin and ochre. A walk in a September meadow might reveal black bears feasting on the huckleberries and elk whistling their mating calls. Here the Tatoosh Range rises above one of the Reflection Lakes near Paradise.

Hoary marmots, so named because of the "hoarfrost" coloration of the fur, find humans fascinating. Members of the woodchuck family, marmots can be heard whistling across the meadows, alerting their neighbors to intruders. They graze in the sub-alpine meadows, lopping off the tops of flowers as if they were cotton-candy puffs.

(overleaf) From the Puget Sound lowlands, Mount Rainier is a prominent landmark. When the mountain wears a lenticular cap, rain or snow usually follows.

SOUTH SOUND

One thing you notice about the Olympia area is the rainbow of wildflowers on the freeway meridian, and the attractive landscaping at interchanges. Another thing you notice is the trees. Hills and lowlands covered with them. But Thurston County, which houses the state capitol in Olympia, is fast converting some of these forests into subdivisions. This enviable location between Seattle and Portland, Oregon, along with proximity to Fort Lewis and patronage by residents of smaller counties to the south, has contributed to the area's popularity.

Governor Mike Lowry has replaced popular Booth Gardner in the Governor's Mansion, and in his first few months oversaw passage of a model state-health-care reform bill, moderated disputes over school reform, and weathered a fight over gay rights legislation. The nearby Evergreen State College continues to turn out liberal arts iconoclasts like Matt Groening ("The Simpsons" creator), playwright and comic strip artist Lynda Barry, and author Stephanie Coontz ("The Way We Never Were") along with actor Michael Richards (who plays Kramer on the TV series "Seinfeld"), co-host of PBS's "This Old House" Steve Thomas, and "Aladdin" animator Michael Swofford. The Evergreen campus, by the way, is buried in acres and acres of trees.

Trees and farms characterize much of the region, where Puget Sound attains its southern reach. Just to the north of Rudd Inlet, it fans out into the wide estuary of the Nisqually River, sheltering migratory waterbirds and nourishing an abundance of wildlife in this unique blend of fresh and salt water. It pokes its fingers toward Shelton, a town that supplies more than three million Christmas trees nationwide.

Beyond the reach of the Sound, pastures and timberlands are punctuated by small towns nearly all the way to Portland. The best scenery is off the backroads, over to Oakville by way of the Capitol Forest (a haven for gourmet chanterelles) and the Mima Mounds Natural Area Preserve.

The Mima Mounds are like blisters on a hairy chest. No one knows for sure what they are, but most geologists believe they are glacial remains. Up to 30 feet wide and seven feet high, the mounds were most probably formed by repeated episodes of freezing and thawing at the end of the Ice Age some 15,000 years ago. Wildflowers, notably blue camas, bloom on these grassy knolls. Many more acres of these pimpled prairies lie outside the preserve in private ownership.

In Olympia's suburb of Tumwater, salmon migrate up the Deschutes River to spawn. With the help of fish hatcheries and ladders, salmon now travel upstream from the previously impassable Tumwater Tells. Fingerlings swim in to Puget Sound, through Admiralty Inlet and the Strait of Juan de Fuca or through the Strait of Georgia, out into the Pacific and up to Alaska, then returning to the river in two to five years and battling their way upstream to begin another generation of wayfarers.

It was in Tumwater that the first permanent settlement of Americans arrived in the region, including the first black man, George Washington Bush. With the burgeoning growth rate of Thurston County, the South Sound region still appears to be a ripe frontier for settlement.

Framed by cherry trees, the Legislative Building in the
state capital of Olympia boasts the tallest dome of any
state capitol. The interior is finished in marble, and the
exterior was constructed of sandstone quarried in
Wilkeson 40 miles to the east.

A lovely waterfall flows past rhododendrons into the Deschutes River at Tumwater Falls Park just south of Olympia. The region's first American settlers arrived in 1845, including a free black man, George Washington Bush.

(right) Hot air balloons ascend at dawn during the Hot Air Fair in Chehalis. The colorful envelopes are inflated first with cool air from fans, then with heated air from propane burners. Balloon ascensions generally occur in early morning and late evening hours when there is little wind.

Aging barns are a common sight in the South Sound region, this one near Chehalis.

(right) The Nisqually Delta National Wildlife Refuge protects the fragile estuary formed where the glacier-born Nisqually River empties into Puget Sound. The twin barns are landmarks on the delta, which is located on the Pacific Flyway and provides a stopover for migrating waterfowl, hawks and owls.

Pumpkins in the field at Oakville, south of Olympia, mean that autumn is nearly over. Children love to visit one of several pumpkin patches in the region to pick out their own jack-o-lanterns.

(right) Autumn burnishes the leaves of the Garry oaks at the Bald Hill Natural Area Preserve near McKenna. The preserve was established to protect the unique native plants found on the dry "balds" of hills in the region. The thin, quick-draining soil supports a grove of lichen-festooned white oaks and native Idaho fescue prairiegrass.

Tacoma's skyline at dawn.

TACOMA/PIERCE COUNTY

This little sister with the homely pulp-mill image is finally getting some respect. Seattle can't help but notice that Tacoma is a competitor to be taken seriously.

First, Tacoma built a dome—the world's largest wooden-domed stadium in 1983, expressive of a spirit that won Tacoma an All-America City award the following year. Then followed renovations: the Pantages Theater. The Rialto and the soon-to-be-completed Theatre on the Square. The Children's Museum of Tacoma and Antique Row—all part of the Broadway Theater District. And the beloved Union Station (now a federal courthouse). A University of Washington branch campus. Artist's lofts. Plans for an upscale Thea Foss Waterway on the industrial tideflats.

Tacoma has lured away Seattle businesses such as Sea-Land Services, Inc., and has attracted high-tech industries and a new Boeing plant. Once-vacant fields backdropped by Mount Rainier are dotted with houses. One drives farther to find the country. In this respect Tacoma is no different from any other growing city. Yet how many places are there where a person can, in a radius of two hours or less, walk in a mountain meadow, night-ski in winter, watch birds on a wildlife refuge, visit a state capitol, drive past tulip and daffodil fields, fish for salmon and watch ocra whales, visit a winery, enjoy Sunday brunch downtown, watch live theatre, and have dinner on the waterfront? Is it any wonder that Puget Sounders are intensely in love with their region?

(opposite) The Green River Gorge cuts through a narrow, fern-covered canyon near Enumclaw.

Backdropped by the Olympics, a bulk carrier takes on a load of grain at Continental Grain Company. The Port of Tacoma exports grains such as corn, wheat and soybeans to markets in Japan, Korea, Saudi Arabia, and India, among others.

Ships loading logs and general cargo dock next to loading cranes at the Port of Tacoma. The port handles 80 to 85 percent of all waterborne commerce from the Pacific Northwest to Alaska, and offers one of the largest Foreign Trade Zones on the West Coast.

A marina on City Waterway is quiet in an October dawn.

Lights, shadows and reflections transform the 1877 Exley Apartments into a painterly portrait of early-day architecture. The building is the only remaining example of a wooden home of its era in downtown Tacoma. It was moved in 1905 from its original location on St. Helens Avenue.

The veil of darkness transforms the mundane into a nightscape of color
and design. The intersection at 12th and A Streets in Tacoma is an artist's
treasure at dawn.

(left) Tacoma was designated an All-America City during its centennial year of 1984. While citizen efforts on behalf of the handicapped and poor were among reasons for the award, the Tacoma Dome and Convention Center, completed in 1983, is the most visible result of the spirit that won the award.

The Dome's blue-patterned roof complements the moods of the Northwest, reflecting the hue of a summer sky or blending with the muted colors of rainclouds and mist. The Dome's quarter-million-dollar neon art by Stephen Antonakos caused a controversy that rivals the battle to change the name of Mount Rainier earlier this century.

Tacoma's skyline is reflected in Thea Foss Waterway. Recent years have seen a boom in construction of new downtown buildings and in restoration of old ones. Once a city in the doldrums, Tacoma is now living up to its nickname as "The City of Destiny." Tacoma was first settled in 1852, and the rival towns of Tacoma and New Tacoma merged into a united Tacoma in 1884.

The Pantages Centre for the Performing Arts, built in 1918, was originally a vaudeville theatre. In 1983, after operating as the Roxy Theatre, it regained its long-lost grandeur after a citizens group spurred a $6 million restoration. The Pantages features world-class entertainment as well as local events such as high-school band concerts.

(right) Mount Rainier backdrops many Pierce County landmarks, Old City Hall among them. Formerly the home of city government, the 1893 Italian Renaissance style brick building now houses offices.

(left) The original Narrows Bridge lasted four months before winds sent the poorly engineered "Galloping Gertie" into a death spasm. The "new" Narrows Bridge, completed in 1950 (a decade after the first span), links the Gig Harbor peninsula with Tacoma.

The Puyallup Valley on a winter morning.

(left) The Seymour Botanical Conservatory at Wright Park is an oasis of life, featuring tropical bromeliads, tree ferns, cacti and orchids as well as seasonal blooms. Land for the park was donated by Charles B. Wright in 1883.

A Douglas fir untouched by early-day saws stands in Chambers Creek canyon near Steilacoom. Preservationists and developers have battled for control of this picturesque canyon, which shelters a salmon hatchery in Tacoma's suburbs.

A "daffy" time is had by all at Tacoma's annual Daffodil Parade. The country's third-largest floral parade, it celebrates the springtime crop of daffodils grown in the Puyallup Valley.

(right) The 12 kilometer (7.4 mile) Sound-to-Narrows race attracts 6500 civilian and 1500 military runners annually. From Vassault Playfield the loop course traverses many hills, including the treacherous "Vassault dip" (seen here) and winds through Point Defiance Park.

The cathedral majesty of a darkwoods forest is at its best during a spring drizzle. Point Defiance Park in Tacoma is a living museum of virgin forest—cedar, hemlock, Douglas fir untouched by early-day logger barons. Some trees are 500 years old. Rhododendron hybrids bloom in May at Point Defiance Park. The wild rhododendron, Washington's state flower, almost lost out to the clover in 1892 when a flower was sought to represent the state.

Wild pink 'rhodies' are most common along the Hood Canal area and in the Olympic Mountains. Washington is now a world leader in the production of ornamental rhododendrons.

(right) The Japanese Gardens at Point Defiance Park are the setting for many weddings. The nearly 700-acre park is bordered on three sides by waterfront.

Restless ducks take wing in October fog above a Flett Dairy Farm pasture in Tacoma.

(right) Fog is the hallmark of Puget Sound autumns. It wraps a landscape in a blanket of pastel, bringing mood and mystery to the commonest path. Strollers in Tacoma's Fort Steilacoom Park sample the quiet pleasures of a foggy dawn. One square mile of the park and adjacent Western State Hospital are on the National Register of Historic Places. A newly restored officer's quarters is one of four of the original military buildings still on hospital grounds.

Northwest Trek Wildlife Park in Eatonville provides a natural habitat for more than 40 species of animals, many free-roaming. Visitors ride a tram through the park to see animals such as elk, mountain goats, desert bighorns, bison and deer.

(right) The Point Defiance Zoo has won national awards for its Pacific Rim theme exhibits, such as this underwater viewing-area for polar bears. Beluga whales, walruses, seals and other aquatic denizens are also housed in see-through tanks. Other animals native to the Pacific shores of North and South America, Asia and Australia live in open displays.

(left) The hamlet of Gig Harbor, just across the Narrows from Tacoma, is the quintessential Puget Sound pastoral, with a quiet harbor, fishing boats, and Mount Rainier in its winter garb.

Fishing boats, Gig Harbor.

(left) The scent is hot and the hounds are off during the Woodbrook Hunt Club Foxhunt on the prairies of Fort Lewis.

Tulips and daffodils were once a popular crop in the Puyallup Valley. Now only a handful of growers farm 400 acres of bulbs. The King Alfred daffodil is the most popular of the 30 varieties grown.

(left) There are few man-made structures that are as picturesque as are barns, and they take on unrivalled character as they age. This pastoral scene is in the Ohop Valley.

Established in 1917 as Camp Lewis, Tacoma's Fort Lewis Army post and nearby McChord Air Force Base employ 8,000 civilians and 32,000 military personnel. Howitzers backdropped by Mount Rainier fire a salute to an incoming commander during a ceremony in front of I Corps Headquarters, Fort Lewis.

Children with painted faces are a common feature of the Western Washington Fair in Puyallup. A down-home country fair on a large scale, the fair draws more than a million visitors who gobble up thousands of chickens, scones and ears of corn on the cob while they "Do the Puyallup" each September.

The oldest incorporated town in the state, Steilacoom (1853) is a placid waterfront community with dozens of New England style homes and buildings. Old-timers and locals frequent the coffee shop of the Bair Drug and Hardware Museum. Visitors can browse through memorabilia while sipping a fountain-fresh malt, ice-cream soda or sarsparilla, or simply enjoying a cup of coffee.

A skier whizzes down the summit of Crystal Mountain, ninety minutes from Tacoma. Crystal Mountain boasts nine chairlifts, 3100 feet of vertical descent, and a cluster of hotels and condos. On New Year's Eve, skiers carry lighted torches down the slopes.

Once or twice in a winter, snow visits the south Puget Sound lowlands, and kids bring out inner tubes and sleds for a ride down the hills. It is rare that the area receives more than a few inches of snow in a single storm, and it usually melts within several days.

(right) The Puget Sound Rain Festival—September to May.

(overleaf) Orb spiders build their lacy palaces in late summer and early autumn. Sometimes hundreds of these dew-covered necklaces will decorate a grassy field or fencerow. French naturalist Jean Henri Fabre commented on the irony of the orb web: "What a refinement of art for a mess of flies!"

SEATTLE

If the story of Seattle were a television series, it would not need embellishment to be a hit. The story comes complete with adventure, drama, hilarity and a cast of characters so colorful that few would believe the story to be fact. The old TV series "Here Come the Brides" was but a pale harvest of the rich fodder of true life as presented by author Bill Speidel, who pricked the balloon of schoolbook history when he wrote his several books about Seattle's founding fathers. Many of our present laws supposedly owe their existence to these men whose wiliness, greed, bravado, hard-headedness, and (where it existed) altruism managed, somehow, to build a city. Arthur Denny, Charlie Terry, Henry Yesler and Doc Maynard, among others, are lionized on street signs.

The First Americans, too, were part of Seattle's history. Through the leadership of peaceloving Chief Sealth (Seattle), the Indian tribes of Puget Sound remained friendly to the whites during the Indian uprisings that followed the hasty, ill-conceived treaty signings of the mid 1850s. Sealth's followers warned villagers of an impending attack by hostile tribes, helping to make the one-day battle of Seattle in 1856 a victory for the pioneers.

Sealth's friendship is especially commendable in light of his horror at having a city named after him. "Doc" Maynard needed a more romantic name for the town; "Duwumps" just didn't cut it. So he stretched his friend's name into the melodious "Seattle" and congratulated himself.

The chief protested, claiming his spirit would grow restless with each mention of his name after his death. Speidel maintains that a businessmen's tax compensated the chief for this future inconvenience and did much to relieve his anxiety. This author would rather follow other writers who ascribe more noble sentiments to Chief Sealth's eventual acceptance of the honor.

Chief Seattle's daughter, Princess Angeline, was one of the most remarkable personages of early-day Seattle. Sometimes wearing a half-dozen dresses at once and cussing a blue streak, she was the original bag lady, loved by residents and tourists alike.

Fledgling Seattle was an unpleasant place to live. The only level land was on an eight-acre island; imposing hills and ravines made construction and travel difficult. Seattle's attributes were mud, fleas, sawdust, mud, odor, bordellos, mud. Untreated sewage spewed back up the pipes with the twice-daily rising of the tide. Potholes were so big that a boy drowned in one. Urban renewal came in the form of the Great Seattle Fire in 1889; a smouldering glue pot laid waste 66 blocks of the pioneer city. Happily, not a single life was lost, and townsfolk began to rebuild before the embers were cool. It was voted to raise the level of homes and shops and to build of brick and stone. City-owned streets were constructed at the decided height, while shopowners too impatient to wait began business at the previous level. The result was like a waffle, on which horses and pedestrians sometimes fell as much as 30 feet from the street to the sidewalk below! As owners filled in and built upward to reach the streets, the buried storefronts became what is now Seattle's Underground—20 square blocks worth underneath Pioneer Square.

Yesler Way in the heart of Pioneer Square was the original Skid Road. On a road of trimmed saplings laid crosswise like railroad ties, running from the forested hills behind the town, logs were skidded to Henry Yesler's sawmill at the waterfront. Over the years, the area became the hangout for the seedy element, and "Skid Road" (or skid row) became synonymous with the down-and-out.

For decades, sawdust from Yesler's mill, ballast from visiting ships, and dirt from regrade projects filled up the potholes and the mudflats. Much of present-day downtown Seattle was once under water at high tide. Regrades lowered many of the town's imposing hills. Old photographs show homes of owners opposed to the regrade perched dozens of feet atop narrow pilings like unearthly hoodoos while the land around them was pressure-hosed away. "So there," said the city. And down, eventually, they came.

The story about the mail-order bride is true. Asa Mercer in 1864 saw a market in the 10,000 virile Puget Sound loggers for feminine comfort of the moral kind. He brought 55 brides in two shipments from back East, but he never realized his goal of bringing over 500 brides and realizing a tidy profit. The bordellos, however, did a booming business.

Seattle is now a modern city of a half million people. It boasts a farmer's and fish market at Pike Place, imposing cathedrals such as Catholic St. James and Episcopal St. Mark's, home-studded hills, dozens of fine art galleries and museums, hundreds of parks and lakes, a zoo with natural habitats, a $26 billion foreign waterborne trade industry, the enormous Boeing Airplane Company, the vast, diversified, manufacturing employer, PACCAR International, miles of salt and freshwater shoreline, a month-long Seafair celebration, burgeoning "suburbs" like Bellevue, swanky hotels such as the Four Seasons Olympic, the computer giant Microsoft Corp., and the Northwest's largest consumer co-op, Recreational Equipment, Inc.

Seattle has made it on numerous "best" lists in the last five years: #1 most livable (*Places Rated Almanac*, Prentice Hall 1989), #2 most livable (*Money* 1990—Bremerton was #1, Tacoma #4 and Olympia #8). #1 U.S. City for Business (*Fortune*). #1 U.S. City for Women (*Savvy*). Second best place to visit (*Conde' Nast Traveler*).

So the truth is out. There *is* life after the Seattle Rain Festival.

Bellevue skyline and Meydenbauer Bay at dusk.

The moving sculpture "Hammering Man" by artist Jonathan Borofsky greets visitors to the new Seattle Art Museum.

Seattle viewed from Harbor Avenue near Alki Beach Park. The Emerald City bears little resemblance to its early days of mud and stilts.

The Space Needle and cityscape from Queen Anne Hill is the city's most popular viewpoint. On a clear evening, tiny Kerry Park may be elbow-to-elbow with photographers.

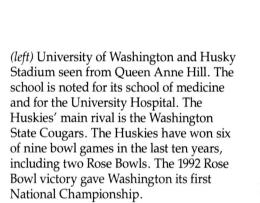

(left) University of Washington and Husky Stadium seen from Queen Anne Hill. The school is noted for its school of medicine and for the University Hospital. The Huskies' main rival is the Washington State Cougars. The Huskies have won six of nine bowl games in the last ten years, including two Rose Bowls. The 1992 Rose Bowl victory gave Washington its first National Championship.

Historic Pioneer Square is a contrast of the old and new, the middle-class and the poor. The picturesque brick buildings were erected after the Great Seattle Fire and were saved from the wrecking ball by preservationists. The wrought-iron park benches are often occupied by "street people." Nearby Yesler Way was Henry Yesler's original 'Skid Road.'

(left) Yoshino cherry trees decorate the Quad at the University of Washington.

Westlake Center, an art deco collection of shops, eateries, and third-story Monorail terminal. Its sunny urban park is a people watcher's' paradise.

Seattle's waterfront boasts seafood eateries, specialty shops and city parks. Until the tideflats were filled in, the present waterfront area was under water at high tide. Colorful banners, hanging baskets, interesting nautical architecture and the ferries make the waterfront a visual treat.

(right) The Kingdome, completed in 1976, is home of the Seattle Seahawks football team and several other national sports teams. The King Street Station tower was built in 1906, copied from the plans of the Campanile in Venice.

Woodland Park's Green Lake is *the* place to go roller-skating, jogging or windsurfing.

(right) The Chinese New Year is celebrated with a Lion Dance through Seattle's International District. Amid drumming and popping firecrackers, the "lion" devours packets of money and cabbage leaves left by storeowners or proffered by children who hope the action rewards them with good luck. The District is widely enjoyed for its shops of exotic merchandise and live poultry and crabs.

(left) Pier 55 Building, Seattle waterfront.

Puget Sound boaters going to and from Lakes Washington and Union must travel through the Government Locks at Ballard (officially known as the Hiram M. Chittenden Locks, but popularly called "the Ballard locks.") Depending on the tide, boats may rise or fall as much as 26 feet when making the transition from fresh to salt water. A fish ladder aids several salmon and trout species in their annual migration to the rivers that empty into Lake Washington.

(*left*) In season, much of Seattle's fishing fleet is offshore, reaping the ocean's bounty of halibut, salmon and king crab. Quaint boats may be seen along the shores of Elliott Bay or moored at Fishermen's Terminal.

A sea captain looks out onto the Sound after bringing his boat to dock along Seattle's waterfront.

The Pike Place Market is alive with colors and saltwater smells as the vendors display an abundance of seafood.

Nets and floats at Fishermen's Terminal—an inadvertent still-life from the sea.

One of the permanent art installations at the new 1.3 mile Metro Bus Tunnel, a collaboration of artists, architects and engineers. $1.5 of the $480 million tunnel project was budgeted for public art, which includes ceramic pieces, tree grates, clocks, neon, the stroboscopic "Saccadoscopoeia" by Bill Bell—where fleeting images are seen only when the eyes move side to side—and this mural by Roger Shimomura.

Microsoft Corporation's headquarters in Redmond. Founded in 1975, Microsoft supplies software for nearly all of the world's 80 million personal computers.

(left) Traditional Japanese dances are performed during the Bon Odori Festival, sponsored by the Seattle Buddhist Church each July. The ceremonial dances are held in the International District a week after the traditional visits to the graves of departed ancestors.

Doc Maynard's Tavern rocks when the sun goes down on Pioneer Square.

(left) Seattle's Woodland Park Zoo is noted for its open-space habitats, and these lions—bored with their old quarters—have moved into the African savannah.

Discovery Park is Seattle's "wild" park. The former Fort Lawton Army post has hundreds of acres of grassy fields that shelter near-tame rabbits. In 1981 a wild cougar was captured in the park. Discovery Park's lighthouse and beaches are a favored place for watching the sunset.

Pike Place Market at Christmas.

With miles of salt and freshwater shoreline, it is natural that Seattle is
home to legions of boaters who tie up in places such as Shilshole Marina.

Dusk along the industrialized Duwamish Waterway is backdropped by the Olympics.

(*right*) Seattle waterfront as the lights come on.

The Boeing Company is the Puget Sound region's largest civilian employer, keeping 80,000 people busy. Founder Bill Boeing's first factory, "The Red Barn," still stands as part of the Museum of Flight. More than half the world's commercial jets have been built at Boeing's plants.

(right) Commuters and vehicles cross the Sound on a system of ferries that connect Seattle with Vashon Island, Bainbridge Island, Bremerton, and Victoria, B.C. Backdropped by the Olympic Mountains, the ferries are an impressive sight. Puget Sound island residents recently rejected a proposal to link islands to the mainland with bridges because of fear the accessibility would destroy the islands' character.

(left) The hill at Gas Works Park is ideal for kite-flying, and some of the fanciest and most outlandish kites have tried their tails in the breeze. The old fixtures of the former gas plant still stand, marked by graffiti. The park, on the shore of sailboat-studded Lake Union, has a 'human sundial'—on which you stand and cast your own shadow—and one of the nicest views of Seattle.

Built for the Century 21 World's Fair in 1962, the Seattle Space Needle is the city's most loved landmark. Featuring a revolving restaurant at the top and a newer lower-level restaurant, the Needle offers an outdoor observation deck with a 360 degree view of the city. The Space Needle is here seen saluted by fireworks during the July 4th celebration.

(overleaf) Evening calm on the Seattle waterfront, with the Olympic Mountains in the distance.

NORTH AND WEST PUGET SOUND

Mount Baker and its neighbor Mount Shuksan are the king and queen of the North Sound region. But it's a funny thing. You don't see Mount Shuksan until you get almost up to it, and Mount Baker's visage from the city of Bellingham 30 miles away is half-hidden, unlike the generous views of Mount Rainier from Tacoma, Seattle and Olympia. Mount Baker's presence is especially imposing, however, when viewed from the Skagit Valley near Mount Vernon where it backdrops barns and quaint steepled churches.

A dormant volcano, Mount Baker is to North Sounders what Mount Rainier is to those in the south. Called Komo Kulshan by the Indians, the "white steep mountain" contains more than thrice the amount of glacier ice as in all of the rest of the United States outside Alaska.

In the mid-1970s, increased thermal activity at the mountain concerned geologists. Steam plumes, dustings of ash, and hot jets of steam and melting ice seemed to signal an impending eruption. The large quantities of hydrogen sulphide being emitted from the vent at Sherman Crater made it one of the region's worst air polluters. The sulphurous odor of rotten eggs can still be detected by hikers at times. The Railroad Grade trail near Schreiber's Meadow brings a hiker close enough to see light puffs of steam from the crater.

Mount Baker has settled down, for the time being, and there are other things to occupy the minds of North Puget Sounders.

Take flowers, for instance.

In spring, the fertile valley around the Skagit River pops with the color of tulips and daffodils. About a thousand acres of farmland are devoted to the production of flower bulbs, and the Mount Vernon area is wising up to the tourist potential of this annual show. Sightseers on a blustery March Sunday almost outnumber the blossoms.

In winter, flocks of snow geese whiten the Skagit valley fields, resting up after the flight from their Siberian breeding grounds. Clots of sandpipers and dunlins share the Skagit flats with the geese; hundreds of these "peeps" rise as if one creature, wheeling, banking, turning like a blowing sheet. Rare trumpeter swans on the farmlands and wintering bald eagles near Rockport also draw birders eager for a glimpse of these symbols of wildness.

Some people in the North Sound region consider themselves more affiliated with the San Juan Islands than with the Puget Sound area in terms of character. Anacortes, for instance, is the jump-off point for the ferry route through this picturesque archipelago. It makes more sense to identify with the mellow, nature-oriented San Juans than with the commercial, populous Tacoma/Seattle/Everett region. But in truth, there is a blending here, just as the Sound itself blends into Admiralty Inlet and the Strait of Juan de Fuca and Rosario Strait and the Strait of Georgia. The northern boundaries are less well-defined. And who cares, anyway?

Away from the waterfront, the flavor is rural: barns from Deming to Snoqualmie, Holstein cows and dairies near Carnation, rows of hip-booted steelheaders on the Skykomish. But the Seattle influence is spreading out. Bucolic towns like Issaquah and Woodinville are sprouting planned residential communities with city-slicker pricetags. Sky-scrapers have hopped Lake Washington and taken root in Bellevue, a mostly upper-crust suburb.

This is a region where hang-gliders sail off 4190 foot Mount Si at North Bend, where skiers hot dog down the lighted slopes at Snoqualmie

Pass, where diners watch the Snoqualmie Falls spill 268 feet into the river's lower reach, where hot-air balloons hang silently in the Snohomish valley, where people tour several of the region's finest wineries.

The Sound also pokes its fingers west of Seattle, forming quiet harbors that didn't go unnoticed by Uncle Sam. In 1891 the Puget Sound Naval Shipyard latched onto the picturesque harbor at Bremerton, where today a fleet of mothballed battleships and carriers lies in dock. The Naval Undersea Warfare Engineering Station is based at Keyport. And in this peaceful setting, backdropped by the Olympic Mountains, lies one of the most controversial spots in the region: Bangor.

Home-port of the Navy's Trident Ohio-class nuclear-powered submarines, capable of firing nuclear weapons, the Naval Submarine Base on Hood Canal has been the target of anti-nuclear activism; but the Tridents, black, silent guardians of defense, employ thousands of people in Kitsap County.

Interestingly, the government with its war machines took special care to preserve as much as possible the natural environment when it poured its concrete. When the base at Bangor was built in 1974, piers were built away from the shoreline so as not to disturb oyster beds and clam areas. The Navy rejuvenated a salmon run that was destroyed in the 1940s when a road closed access to Devil's Hole Lake. The Trident support piers have a unique system of collecting grease, debris and other matter, not allowing it to wash into Hood Canal. The base houses a full-time game warden, forester and marine biologist.

The West Sound region is also a blend of cultures, represented by the Scandinavian town of Poulsbo and the Indian village of Suquamish. The fair-skinned Norwegian descendants raise a 'Midsommar' Pole each year to celebrate their heritage; the Indians host Chief Seattle Days to commemorate theirs.

Members of tribes throughout the West join the Suquamish on the Port Madison Indian Reservation in August for a pow-wow of dancing, feasting and canoe racing. "Once," lamented an Indian during the 75th celebration of Chief Seattle Days, "little Boy Scouts with blond hair and blue eyes did Indian dances while we watched." Now it is truly an Indian event. Salmon is prepared as in days gone by, split and bound by tongs of green wood, hissing like cobras' heads around an alder fire. Young men and women paddle war canoes across the blue waters of their ancestors, with the Space Needle and the Columbia Center in the background.

It was the Suquamish who first saw British Captain George Vancouver sail into the Sound in 1792. And it was Chief Sealth who played a key role in the growth of the Puget Sound region. An eloquent orator, a staunch defender of peace, a friend of the whites, a Christian who honored in his own way the Great Tyee, Chief Seattle has an honored position in the region's history.

But it is a bittersweet honor. The signing of the treaty that gave much of his people's land to the white race in the mid-1850s was, he felt, inevitable. Though recent scholarship questions the authenticity of his eloquent and oft-quoted speech, Chief Seattle's words as tradition retells them ring true down the generations. "My people are few," he told Governor Isaac Stevens. "They resemble the scattering trees of a storm-swept plain.... There was a time when our people covered the land as waves of a wind-ruffled sea cover its shell-paved floor.... (But) tribe follows tribe, and nation follows nation, like the waves of the sea. It is the order of nature, and regret is useless."

Standing on the knoll where the burial canoes rise above the Christian tombstone, the breeze ruffling the flowers left to grow wild, you can hear the old chief speak from the land he once hunted.

"Every part of this soil is sacred to my people. Every hillside, every valley, every plain and grove has been hallowed by some sad or happy event in days long vanished.... When your children's children shall think themselves alone in the fields, the store, the shop, upon the highway, or in the silence of the pathless woods, they will not be alone.... These shores will swarm with the invisible dead of my tribe."

The Lake Whatcom Railway steam train pulls into Wickersham junction. The engine, built in 1907, formerly ran on coal as a switch engine, hauling rail cars to factories in Tacoma and Seattle. Now powered by an oil burner, it takes tourists, and in December Santa Claus, on a 6-mile nostalgia trip through the countryside.

(left) Bringing home the Christmas tree, Mount Baker Recreation Area.

Mount Baker looms above the Fir-Conway Lutheran Church near Mount Vernon.

(*left*) Alpenglow colors Mount Shuksan
at sunset.

A red-wing blackbird challenges a spring
fog at the Blue Heron Marsh in Auburn.
Formerly a gravel pit, the marsh now
claims a blue heron rookery in the tall
alders, within sight of two freeways.

The old Dalby Mill at Union on Hood Canal furnished electricity in the 1920s. Now rotted and unmaintained, the mill will likely become part of the forest humus.

The Boeing Commercial Airplane Group's Assembly Plant at Everett is the largest building by volume in the world. It houses assembly for the Boeing 747 and 767, rolling out five of each every month. A 1993 expansion increased the size by 50 percent to accommodate the new 777, slated to enter service in 1995. Nearly 100,000 visitors tour the plant each year.

Courtesy Boeing Commercial Airplane Group

(left) When the Hood Canal Floating Bridge blew down in a storm in 1979, the Lofall-South Point ferry was put back in service linking the Olympic peninsula with the Puget Sound region. Now that the bridge has been rebuilt, the *Klahowya* runs between Fauntleroy and Vashon Island.

The fishing village of LaConnor with Mount Baker. Saltwater smelt runs bring out the "jiggers" in mid-winter along the Swinomish Slough.

(left) The 1906 Mukilteo Lighthouse is adjacent to the ferry terminal. Nearby Everett was the smelter site for early-day gold and silver mines at Monte Cristo in the North Cascades.

A winter sun rises over the Snohomish River near Everett.

Poulsbo celebrates its Scandinavian heritage with a Midsommar Fest. Costumed participants and spectators dance a broad circle around the greens-decked midsummer pole for the 100th anniversary of the town's settlement by Norwegian immigrants.

(right) Sailboaters find good racing weather on Puget Sound. The Whidbey Island Race Week draws more than 100 spinnaker-outfitted boats each summer.

Bellingham's Whatcom Museum of History and Art was built in 1892 as the city hall for New Whatcom. The town later merged with other townships to form Bellingham. Museum exhibits include a turn-of-the-century bedroom, parlor and child's playroom and logging and Northwest Coast Indian artifacts.

(*right*) A salmon trawler prepares for the Anacortes Christmas Boat Parade.

(left) Winter is the time that dunlins, western sandpipers and other shorebirds gather along the Skagit River delta. Siberian snow geese winter over at the Skagit flats as well.

Islands and mountains rise on the horizon of Bellingham Bay. Bellingham hosts a Ski to Sea Relay each May, with 200 teams (some from as far away as Japan) racing on skis, foot, bicycle, canoe and catamaran 70 miles from the slopes of Mount Baker to Bellingham Bay.

(*left*) The Skagit Valley bursts into color in spring. More than a thousand acres of tulips, daffodils and irises lure visitors to witness the event. There is no truth to the rumor that Mount Vernon ships its bulbs to Holland, although it *is* one of the world's largest tulip-growing regions.

Indian youths dressed in native costume perform traditional dances at the Chief Seattle Days celebration in Suquamish. Chief Seattle's grave lies not far from the little town, overlooking, across the Sound, the city that bears his name.

Dusk on Puget Sound.